WHEN EVEN THE COWS WERE UP

Kate's Book of Childhood in the Early 1900s and After

by
Kate Pedigo

Megan Holbrook, Editorial Coordinator

Kate Pedigo

MIDMARCH ARTS PRESS
New York   1990

MIDMARCH ARTS BOOKS

The Little Cat Who Had No Name
Artists and Their Cats
The Lady Architects: Howe, Manning and Almy, 1893–1937
Camera Fiends and Kodak Girls: 50 Selections by and about Women in Photography 1840–1930
Yesterday and Tomorrow: California Women Artists
No Bluebonnets, No Yellow Roses: Texas Women in the Arts
Pilgrims and Pioneers: New England Women in the Arts
Whole Arts Directory
Women Artists of the World
Voices of Women: 3 critics on 3 poets on 3 heroines
American Women Artists: Works on Paper
Guide to Women's Art Organizations and Directory for the Arts

Copyright © 1990 Kate Pedigo
Published by Midmarch Arts Press
All Rights Reserved

Printed in the United States
Library of Congress Catalog Card Number: 90-71867
ISBN: 1-877675-06-7

design: Two Lip Art
typographic design: Barbara Bergeron

Copies of this book may be obtained from:
Midmarch Arts Books
Box 3304 Grand Central
New York, NY 10163

CONTENTS

Introduction
Before Kate Was Born
    Tex's Family
    Kate's Family
    A Bicycle Built for Two
    Riding on the Streetcar
    After the Ball Game
Kate Growing Up
    Waiting Up for 10 O'Clock
    Putting Salt on the Robin's Tail
    A Cold New Home for Kate
    The Pet Chickens
    The Tree House
    "Give Me the First Kiss, Daddy"
    Armistice Day
    Extra, Extra!
    Moving the House on Logs
    Threading the Needle for Grandma
    Every Sunday Morning
    Christmas Eve
    High Top Shoes and Stilts
    Sliding Down the Bannister
    Even the Cows Are Up
    The Garage
    Riverboats
    "Glad It Wasn't Me"
    Kate's First Date
    The World's Fair
    Ohio River Flood
All Grown-up
    "More Coffee Please"
    Company Picnic and Egg Toss
    The Costume Party
    Miss Maisano's Class
Biography — About Kate
Photo Album
Song Lyrics
    "My Old Kentucky Home," "Tiger Rag," "Beautiful Ohio," "Back Home Again In Indiana"

INTRODUCTION

Kate Pedigo didn't start to study art until she was almost 60 years old. Then she realized immediately that the drawing she enjoyed so much was a way of capturing and sharing the memories of her lifetime.

****

This book tells in story and drawing what it was like growing up in the early part of the 20th century. In that gentler day, entertainments and games were simpler and mostly within the home. Families spent a lot of time together. They enjoyed just sitting on the porch on summer evenings watching for shooting stars and counting fireflies.

Kate saw enormous changes during her life — horse-drawn buggies gave way to Model-T's and then to increasingly complicated and fancy cars. Roads that were only one lane wide (you had to pull over to let an oncoming car pass) became eight-lane superhighways. When Kate was young, the daily papers were the only source of news. There was no television; there were no anchor men to sum up events each evening; no VCRs; and there certainly was no flying to Europe for a weekend jaunt.

Each of Kate's drawings in this book tells a story of an event or memory that she cherishes. They are to be colored in the way you think Kate meant them to look. She began making these drawings of her memories of childhood for Christmas cards to send to friends.

Tex's Family

In 1892, Delitha, her husband Sam, and her two sons moved from Virginia to the Texas Panhandle in a covered wagon, where they became homesteaders. This meant that they had to live on the land for a certain number of years and cultivate it, and then finally could claim it as theirs. The family lived in a dugout house (a house built into a hillside and with a dirt floor) for several years before they built one from wood. Delitha cooked their meals over the fire in the fireplace. She picked cotton, milked cows, churned butter, killed snakes, did the cooking, washing, ironing, sewing, gardening and many other chores.

Her husband Sam was a part-time Texas Ranger, farmer, horse trader, and for a while sold gravestones and fruit trees all around the country.

One of her sons, Tex, did a lot of traveling after he left home and eventually settled in Los Angeles. It was there he met Kate, when she was all grown up and on a vacation trip, and married her some three months later.

Delitha Cassandrew Jackson Pedigo, Pioneer Lady, 1893

Kate's Family

Edna Burr and John Howison Meet at an Elocution Contest

Edna Burr and John Howison, Kate's parents, met in 1900 at an elocution contest in church. Edna, Kate's mother, had studied both piano and the art of elocution, which involved reading in front of an audience. She was reciting a poem in the church contest, and forgot one of the verses in the middle of it. She quickly made one up and recited it. To her surprise, she won the contest. John Howison, Kate's father, was in the audience, and after the contest asked the minister to introduce them. The couple was married two years later.

A Bicycle Built for Two

Kate's mother often entertained her children by telling them stories of riding with their father on his old tandem bike. A tandem bike is a bicycle that two people can ride on, and it was very practical in those days. It cost less than a horse and buggy, and did not have to be fed and rubbed down like a horse. Kate's father and a friend of his used the bicycle to go to work every day. He also took Kate's mother out for rides. She enjoyed bicycling very much, but it scared her because they nearly had several accidents with horse drawn buggies. To ride the bicycle, Kate's mother had to wear a divided skirt, like pants, but much fuller in the legs. She thought these were quite revealing and was a little embarrassed to wear them. Women soon began to wear bloomers instead. These were big, fluffy pants that ended below the knee and were much more practical for bicycle riding. Women kept their hats on by pinning them to their hair, which they wore in a big bun on top of their head.

Riding on the Streetcar

When Kate's mother and father were still courting, they went for a ride on a streetcar one Sunday. The Chicago Streetcar company offered their horse-drawn streetcars for charter on Sunday afternoons. It was winter and some boys started to throw mudballs at the car. Kate's mother laughed because she thought this was funny. When one of the mudballs landed in her mouth, she didn't think it was so funny anymore.

Streetcars then were different in every city because they could be ordered custom-made. Some cars used four horses instead of two, and some were double-deckers. In Ontario, California, a streetcar line went all the way up a hill. The horse would pull it to the top, then the driver would put the horse on the car, and they would coast back down the hill.

When Kate was young, the streetcars were powered by electricity. A steel rod ran from the top of the streetcar to an overhead power line that ran the length of the tracks. Young boys used to try to dislodge this rod by jumping up and down on the back of the cars. Occasionally, they would succeed in jarring the rod loose from the line and the motorman would have to get out and fix it.

After the Ball Game

Kate's father, who loved sports, played golf and baseball. One day when he and Kate's mother and baby Ethleen (their first-born child) were going home from a baseball game, Ethleen started crying, and would not stop. The young parents were so embarrassed by the noise that they walked all the way home in alleys so they would not see anyone.

When Kate's family moved to Indiana, her father's company started a baseball team, and he was the manager. Kate would go to baseball games all the time. She enjoyed watching players getting caught between bases, and of course she loved home runs. However, she hated sitting through double headers, when the team would play two games in a row. That was too much baseball for Kate.

The *Courier Journal*, the leading newspaper in Louisville, maintained a light board outside the stadium. There was an outline of a baseball diamond on the board, with a light bulb showing each of the bases. As the newspaper received news by telephone of the World Series' Games, they would light the bases where the players were. They also announced the score with lights. This was before radio and T.V. — people who watched the board were fascinated by the instant news "flashes."

Waiting Up for 10 O'Clock

When Kate was five years old, she wanted very badly to see what it would be like to stay up late. She had heard her parents talk about being up until 10 p.m. and she begged them to let her stay up that late. They finally agreed. That night Kate sat at the table with Ethleen and her parents, waiting for 10 o'clock. Ethleen was reading a book. Her father was smoking a cigar and playing cards with her mother. Kate got sleepier and sleepier and finally dozed off, still sitting at the table. Her mother and father woke her up just before the clock struck 10 so that she could see what staying up late felt like; then they sent her to bed.

At the time, Kate's house still had gas lights that were lit with matches. The gas was regulated by a meter on the outside of the house. Every time the lights went low, it meant they had to put another quarter in the meter.

Kate's mother had a wooden washing machine. To wash the clothes, she would push the wooden crossbar back and forth.

To use the telephone, Kate's mother would turn the little handle around rapidly. This connected her to the operator, who would get her the number she was calling. It was a privilege for Kate to be allowed to talk on the phone. Once in a while her mother would stand her up on a high chair in front of the phone and allow her to talk to her father or a neighbor. Kate found this very exciting.

"waiting up to see what 10 o'clock is like"

Putting Salt on the Robin's Tail

When mother thought it was time for her girls to go outdoors for some fresh air, she bundled them up in coats, mufflers and caps, gave each a salt shaker and told them to put salt on the robin's tail. One day, after trying and failing to get close enough to the robins, the girls went back indoors feeling very discouraged. Kate told mother she was giving up. Ardell, Kate's younger sister, got an inspiration and called out, "try pepper!"

This story may sound strange to city children, but Kate's friend, who grew up in Oklahoma, was also sent outdoors by his mother with instructions to put salt on the robin's tail.

A Cold New Home for Kate

In 1917, when Kate was six years old, she and her family moved from Joliet, Illinois, to New Albany, Indiana. Her father had gotten a job with the railroad in Louisville, Kentucky, but he couldn't find a house there. Finally, after several months of searching, he found a small house in New Albany, which was just across the river from Louisville. The house had been built for people to use in the summer and was not well insulated. The first winter in New Albany was very cold and snowy. Kate and her sisters, who had to sleep upstairs in unheated bedrooms, would leave their long underwear in front of the stove every night, so in the morning it would be toasty warm. Father built such big fires in the coal stove that at times it would turn red-hot and blister the paint right off the wall.

In this picture, Kate and her sisters, Ethleen and Ardell, are getting dressed, Father is bringing in the coal, and mother is rocking the baby, Ruth, to sleep. The table is set for breakfast near the stove so everyone can stay warm.

The Pet Chickens

Kate's family kept chickens in New Albany so they would have lots of eggs to eat. Kate and Ardell each kept one of the chickens as her special pet. Since the chickens were Rhode Island Reds, the pets were called Reddy and Rhoddy. Sometimes the girls would put doll clothes on their pets, though it was difficult to get the chickens to stay in them. Other times they would trade pets with each other, then charge each other a nickel to trade back.

Kate and her sisters also dressed up their dolls, played jacks and marbles, and built all sorts of things with tinkertoys. At Christmas, Kate would sometimes get a wind-up toy with wheels and a key on the bottom. When she turned the key it would wind up a spring inside the toy; then when she set the toy on its wheels, it would run around on the floor. Once, Kate wound the spring too tight and the toy broke.

The Tree House

When Kate was in first grade, there was a scarlet fever epidemic in her town. Scarlet fever was very contagious and when children got it, they had to be quarantined, that is, kept home from school so as not to expose the other children. That year so many children caught scarlet fever that all the schools closed down and the children had to stay home. During the quarantine, Kate's sister Ethleen would go sit in the treehouse she shared with the boy who lived next door. They both loved to read and would stay up in the treehouse all day reading books. Kate longed to go up and join them. She even brought a book to read, but her sister said she was too young to be admitted.

"Give Me the First Kiss, Daddy"

One day Kate and her family moved into a larger house closer to the center of town. The children waited each night for their father to come walking up the sidewalk towards home. Then they would burst out the door and run up to him shouting, "Give me the first kiss, Daddy!" Ethleen usually got to him first because she had the longest legs. In winter the children would gang up on their father at the front door and he would give them all frosty bear hugs.

In the summer, all the neighborhood children would gather in front of Kate's house to play hide and seek and other games. The sidewalks were made of cinder and very rough. Kate fell down once and hurt her knee badly, but her father bandaged it and it healed quickly.

The family would sit out on the porch on summer evenings and watch falling stars. Kate's father would sit in a rocking chair and put his feet up on the bannister. On a clear night, the Milky Way would shine across the sky like a white ribbon.

Armistice Day

On November 11, 1918, World War I ended; this is the day we now call Armistice Day. When Kate's mother heard the news, she bundled up Ardell, put Ruth in the buggy with a bunch of pan lids and big spoons, and she walked to Kate's school to tell everyone the wonderful news. Kate's school only had two teachers; each of them taught two grades, and they would teach the two grades in the same room. When Kate's mother got there, she passed out the pan lids and spoons and told the children to make a lot of noise. The children had a great time banging on them and shouting that the war was over. Kate's mother was especially pleased because her brother was in the Navy and this meant that he would be coming home.

The post office sold victory stamps to celebrate the end of the war. Kate and her sisters would paste stamps in a book, and when it was full, they could take the book back to the post office and turn it in for a bond.

Extra, Extra!

During Kate's childhood, telephone, telegraphs, and newspapers were the only source of news. People who lived out in the country and didn't have phones had to wait until their newspapers were delivered to find out what was happening in the world. Kate's father read three newspapers a day: *The Courier Journal*, *The New Albany Tribune*, and another Louisville paper. He would often fall asleep reading one of the newspapers, but would never admit it, saying he was just resting his eyes.

The paper boy delivered the newspapers in the afternoon; he always looked very small to be carrying two heavy bags of newspapers. When something important or exciting happened, the paper would print an extra edition. This would be rushed to the newsboys, who would then go up and down the streets calling out "Extra! Extra! Read All About It!" People would run out of their houses to get a copy.

Kate was still young when the radio was invented. Her friend Mary Jane, who lived up the street, had a brother who was one of the first people in the neighborhood to get a crystal set, the early type of radio. Sometimes Mary Jane would invite Kate up to listen. One person would put on a set of headphones and then move a connecting wire around on a lump of metal, which was called a crystal. Whoever was lucky would hear a bit of music or someone talking.

Moving the House on Logs

At home, Kate loved to sit in the bay window seat and watch traffic and people go by outside. One day, she was very surprised to see a house go by. A group of men and a truck were moving a house down the street on logs. The logs were like ends of telephone poles, about two or three feet long. The truck would roll the house forward, and the men would pick up the logs from the back of the house and bring them up to the front. Then they would slip the logs underneath the house so it could keep rolling along. Historians tell us that the pyramids, which were built with huge blocks of stone, were constructed with this same technique for moving the blocks.

Threading the Needle for Grandma

When Grandma visited Kate and her family, she usually stayed for several weeks. She would help Kate's mother by sewing for the family. One day when Kate was nine, she told her mother that she wanted to sew. Her mother said she was foolish to want to learn so young, but gave Kate some pieces of cloth to sew. Kate sewed them together so quickly, her mother was very surprised. She didn't know that Grandma had taught Kate to sew. Later, Grandma also taught her how to make patterns, and from then on Kate made most of her own clothes.

In the early 1900s, ladies often wore gimps like the one Grandma is wearing in this picture. Gimps were ornamental pieces of embroidery, stiffened with net and wire so they would stay up under the chin. They came up high around the neck and went down to the waist where they were tied with a little ribbon. Ladies wore their dresses over the gimps.

In the picture, the sewing machine is by the window. This was a "treadle machine" made before sewing machines were motorized. To sew, Kate would push the treadle (the part that says SINGER) back and forth with her feet. That made the needle move up and down to stitch the cloth.

Every Sunday Morning

Every Sunday morning, Daddy went to work at the railroad, Kate and her siblings went to Sunday school, and Mother prepared Sunday dinner. As soon as Daddy got home, he would sit in his big chair with the four younger children gathered round and read the "funnies." There was only one electrical socket in the whole house, and only one lamp, so reading together was the best way for everyone to see the comics. If Daddy was out of town, Ethleen would read instead. Kate and her sisters and brother liked the Katzenjammer Kids the best.

"Every Sunday Morning"

Christmas Eve

In Southern Indiana, most people went to the timber-covered hills to cut their Christmas trees, though the local grocery store sold nice trees for about $1.25. The tree Kate's father got was so tall it almost touched the ceiling. The family would trim the tree together and play classical music on a record player — called a Victrola.

Kate and her sisters waited with great anticipation for Christmas and Santa Claus's visit. Once, about 2 a.m. on a Christmas Eve, Kate's sister Ardell noticed light coming from downstairs and sneaked down to see if Santa Claus had already come. Ethleen and her parents were in the kitchen wrapping presents for the younger children. Apparently Santa Claus had been so quiet they hadn't heard him or seen him leave his presents. Ardell saw the matching baby carriages and doll clothes for herself and Kate, the tennis racquet for Ethleen, and Monopoly and checkers for the whole family. She crept quietly back to bed and told Kate what Santa Claus had brought.

High Top Shoes and Stilts

When Kate was 12, Mother took the three younger girls to the shoe store before school started. She bought each girl a pair of all-leather high-top shoes. Each pair cost $7.00. Mother wanted the girls to wear high-top shoes because she thought that would keep their ankles trim. The store owner gave each girl a pair of wooden stilts with steps adjustable for three heights. Grandma taught them how to walk on the stilts.

Boys in the early 1900s wore pants strapped at the knee with buckles. These were called knickers. The boy who lived next door, Robert Emmett McDowell, refused to buckle his knickers because he thought if they hung loose he would look older. He built a scooter out of boards and skate wheels. Most boys had these scooters and some even put wooden boxes behind the handles for storage.

Aunt Jean, father's sister, gave the girls a tent to play in. They had no tentpole, so Mother would hang the tent over the clothesline. Kate's little brother Donnie loved to keep cool in the summer playing with his duck and sailboat in a tub of water. On the clothesline in this picture are two old-fashioned bathing suits that Kate and her sisters used to wear.

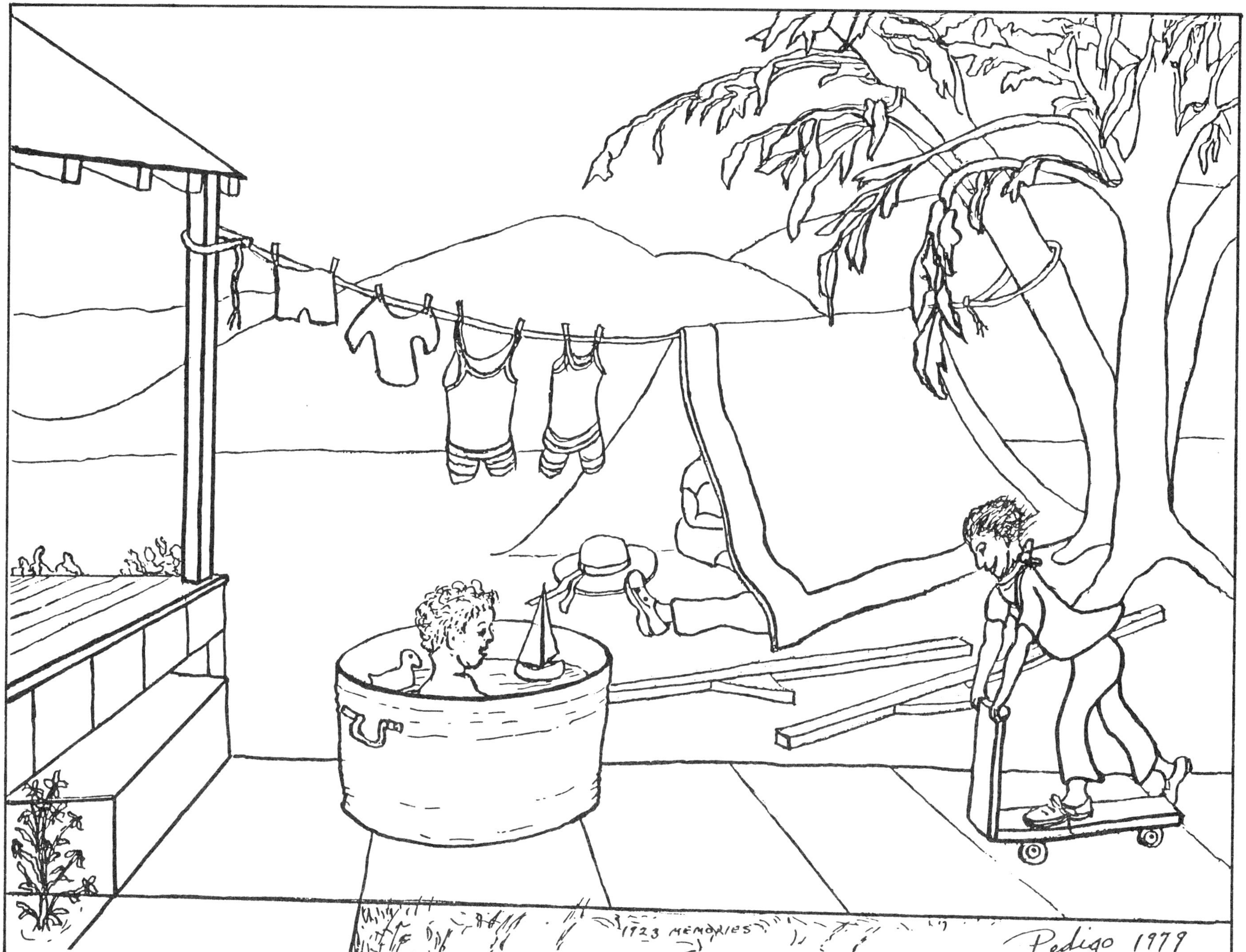
1923 MEMORIES
Pedigo 1979

Sliding Down the Bannister

Kate's teacher in sixth grade, Mr. Hester, taught her class on the second floor of the school. He was also the principal and when students were bad they were sent to Mr. Hester. One day a boy brought in a note. Mr. Hester read it silently and then took his paddle out of the drawer to spank the boy for what he had done. He took the boy outside the classroom to give him the punishment, and bent him over the bannister of the stairs to paddle him. However, the boy slipped out of reach and slid down the bannister. Mr. Hester hit the bannister instead of the boy, and broke the paddle to bits. The boy ran home, and Mr. Hester went back into the classroom with his face as red as a beet.

SILVER STREET SCHOOL
New Albany, Indiana

SILVER STREET SCHOOL
1922

Even the Cows Are Up

Kate's family owned a big black Model-T Ford. It was a railroad company car given to Kate's father during a railroad strike so he could get to work more easily. The luggage rack held the luggage on the side. There was a running board people had to step on to get into the car. The rides were very bumpy. In winter, Kate's father would put up thick black curtains with little glassine windows to keep out the cold. The windshield wiper was only on the driver's side and was operated by a little handle the driver turned to get the wiper to move back and forth. The car had a very shiny brass radiator grille.

When Kate was 13, she and her entire family went on a visit to her mother's aunts and uncle in central Illinois, about 175 miles from New Albany. They had to get up at 5:30 in the morning. Ardell was surprised that cows were already in the pastures, and she exclaimed, "Even the cows are up!"

One of Mother's aunts operated a small hotel, and the Howison family visited them for a few days. Kate and her sisters were very excited because they had never spent the night in a hotel. They were allowed to eat in the hotel restaurant, a room with wooden straight-backed chairs and tables. The hotel was very near the railroad, and many traveling salesmen, who were called "drummers," stayed here. They had heavy cases filled with samples of whatever they were selling and a few stopped to show Kate their wares. Kate and her family also stayed with another of her mother's aunts at her house in Bloomington, Illinois. This was a large house, encircled by a great big porch. The family owned a farm where the dirt was black as coal. For breakfast, Kate's great-aunt fried a huge platter of eggs, much more than Kate's family could eat, because she was used to cooking for the farmhands, who ate an enormous amount of food.

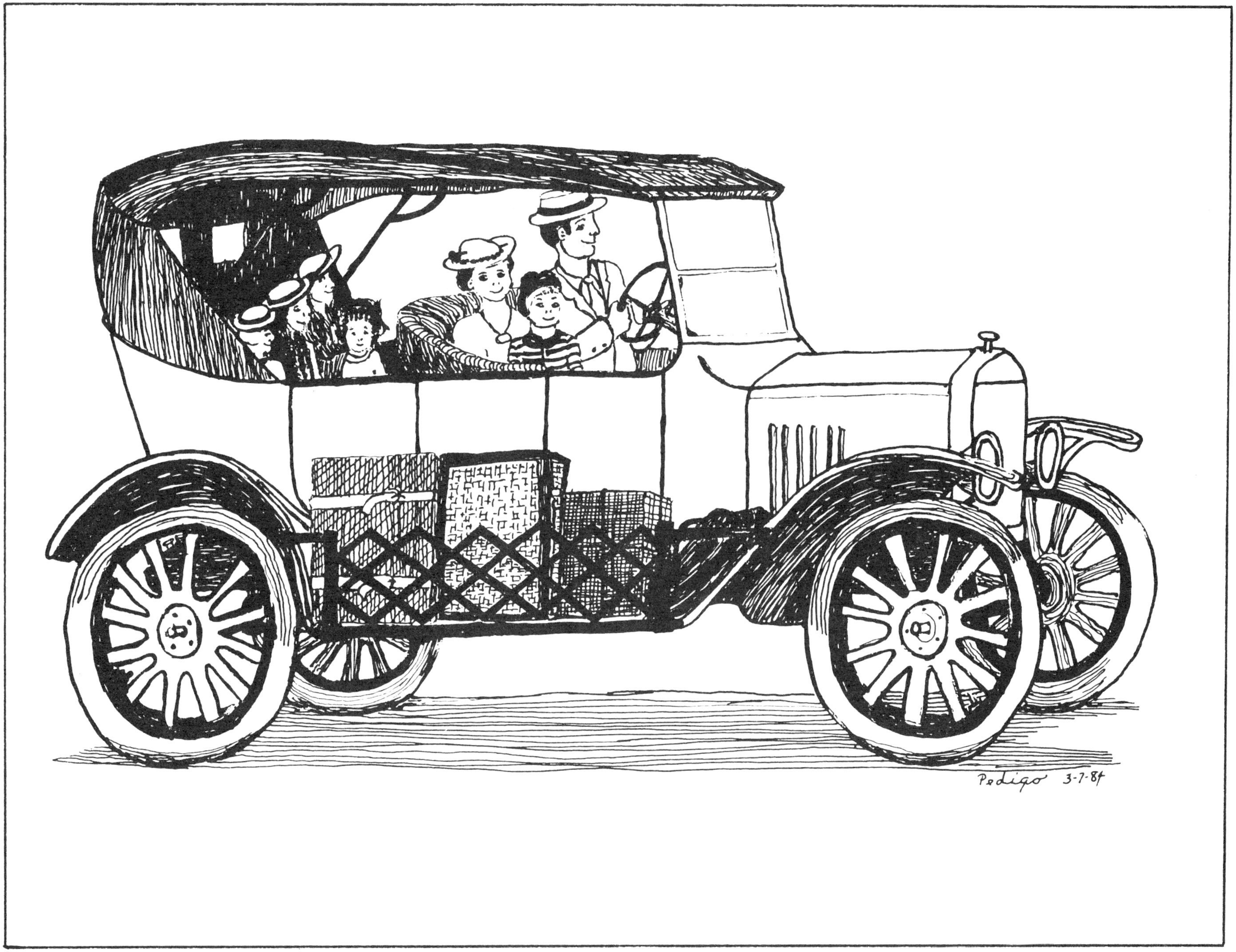
Pedigo 3-7-84

The Garage

When Kate's father owned his Model T, service stations were very different from today. They were usually small buildings or stores with a single gasoline pump out front. The owner of the service station would pump the gas from a holding tank to a ten-gallon glass tank at the top of the pump by working a metal handle back and forth (ten times for each gallon). Then he would put the nozzle of the hose into the car tank and gravity would force the gas down into it. Sometimes gas was as cheap as seven cents a gallon. Oil was kept in glass bottles with a metal spout at the top for pouring. Garages were very simple in the early days and it was a lot less expensive to fix a car. Tires were thinner and had punctures more often, so there was a lot of tire repair work. There was a garage in Louisville that advertised "Invite us to your next blowout." This drawing is of a cartoon that Kate remembers from a newspaper in the 1920s.

Service stations were not usually equipped with rest rooms like they are now. Travelers would have to stop by the side of the road or find a church or school with an outhouse. Most of the roads that cars could use were unpaved dirt or gravel roads which were very dusty in the summer, and muddy or impassable in the winter. Some were called crown roads. These were built so that the center of the roads was higher than the sides. Rain water would run off more easily, so there would be less mud. In the parts of Illinois where Kate and her family traveled, half the road would be paved with brick. They would drive along on the brick side until another car came towards them. Depending on who had the right of way, one of the cars would have to pull over onto the dirt side until the other had passed. At one point, the road went across a farm. The farmer charged a toll to drive over his property.

Memories of an early 1920's cartoon.   Pedigo 85

Riverboats

During her childhood, Kate went on many riverboat trips on the Ohio River, a very popular outing. Her church group would charter a riverboat for the day and everyone would pack a picnic lunch. Kate would wait excitedly on the dock for it to arrive. Everyone would walk across the gangplank onto the boat. Kate and her friends would have fun running around the decks and up and down the stairs. On the first deck musicians would play. This was the age of Ragtime music, and everyone loved to hear the "Tiger Rag." There was a large dance floor with seats around it to sit and watch people dance the Charleston. Sometimes the boat would also have a calliope, an organ run by steam, which would play many kinds of music.

The riverboat would arrive at a park on the bank of the river, where it would dock, and everyone would debark. They would unpack their lunches and picnic. Then the children would play and the adults would snooze. After a few hours, everyone would reboard the boat and head back to New Albany. The riverboats burned coal to make the steam that turned the paddle wheels and the smoke from the coal was very sooty. By the end of the day, Kate's face would be very, very dirty.

Sometimes Kate and her family would take boat trips in the early evening. These were called "sunsets" because they traveled down the river to see the beautiful sunsets that were common in the area. After the sun set, the boat would return to town.

Most church group meetings on the boats ended with everyone singing favorite old songs like "Beautiful Ohio," "Back Home In Indiana," and "My Old Kentucky Home."

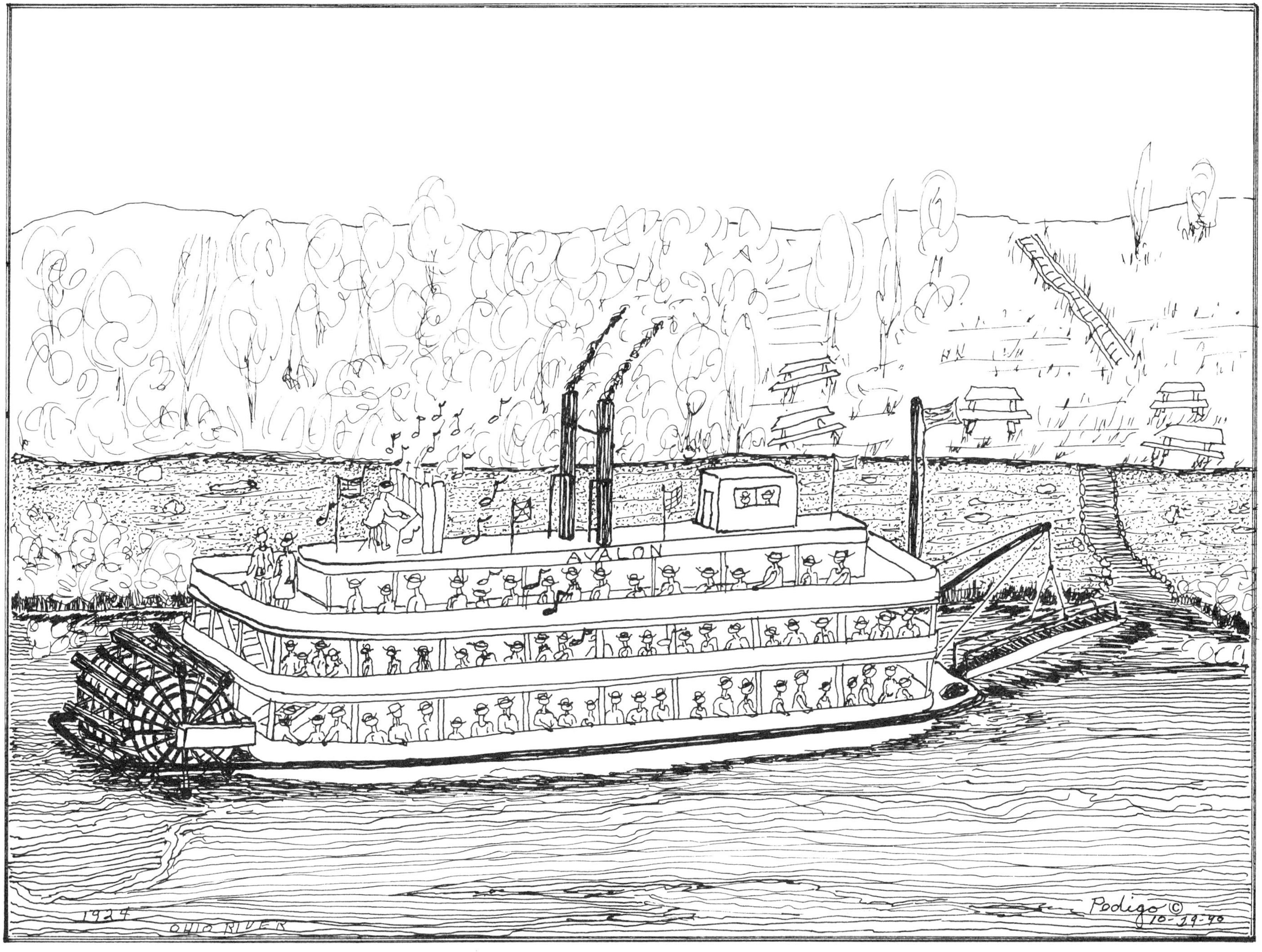
AVALON
1924
OHIO RIVER
Podigo ©
10-19-90

"Glad It Wasn't Me"

Kate's mother took orders for the supper menu from the Birthday Person. Of course the choice was always cake and ice cream. Kate learned to bake when she was about nine years old. Everyone raved about her cakes. She even made birthday cakes for her grandmother and her aunts and uncle which her mother would package and mail to Chicago.

One time when her brother Don was very small, a cake was cooling on the kitchen table. Don stuck the candles in the hot cake; of course, they melted. After the cake cooled, Kate dug the paraffin lumps out and filled the holes with frosting. Then she frosted the rest of the cake.

The family always had a white tablecloth. Mother didn't like colored ones or the oil cloth so many of Kate's friends' mothers used. Each child had a chair of a different height so they would be comfortable sitting at the table.

Whenever one of the children turned over a glass of water or milk, father would always say "Glad it wasn't me." Then each person would say "Glad it wasn't me" all the way around the table. Father was always joking and laughing. He served the food, fixing the youngest children's plates first, cutting up their meat, and scraping corn off the cob. He told stories about his daily activities, which included visiting factories. The children's favorite was his description of a cookie factory and the cookies on a conveyer belt.

There was a metal icebox in the kitchen. As the ice in it melted, the water went through a tube and into a flat pan under the box that had to be emptied regularly. At times it was neglected and ice water would run all over the kitchen. Some people bored a hole in the floor under their ice box. The water would flow into a funnel in the hole, then through a little pipe and down into the basement to a drain.

"GLAD IT WASN'T ME"

Kate's First Date

In the summer before Kate entered high school, she and her friend Martha Jane Welsh went to the Soldiers and Sailors Cemetery for a Memorial Day dedication. At the ceremonies they met two boys about their own age, Julius Hock and Paul Trudeau. The four talked together for a long time. When Kate got home that day, Julius called on the phone to ask if he could pay a visit. The visit was very nice and for the rest of the summer Kate and Julius double-dated with Martha and Paul. The dates consisted of long walks, swinging in the porch swing, and playing mah jong and checkers. At the close of the summer, Kate and Julius had a misunderstanding. It was the end of their friendship, and throughout the rest of high school they never spoke a word to one another again.

At Kate's 50th high school reunion, she and Julius finally had a long chat. They now write to one another from time to time. It was Julius who suggested that Kate draw a picture of their first date more than 50 years ago. She drew them sitting in the porch swing. With mosquitoes buzzing around them and the scent of rambler roses filling the air, they talked for hours and hours.

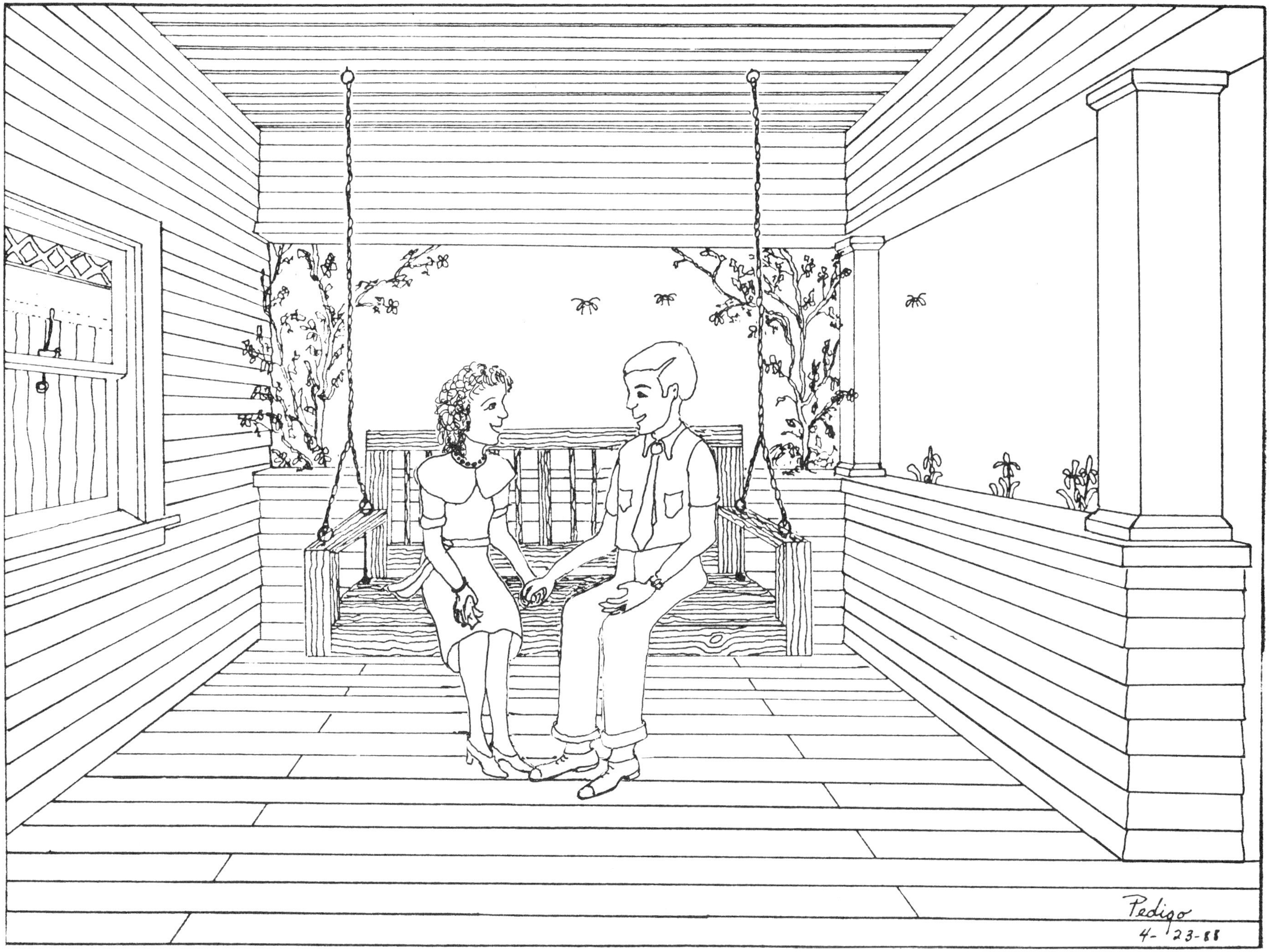
Pedigo
4-23-88

The World's Fair

The World's Fair still takes place every few years in a different city somewhere in the world. Participants come from all over to show inventions and sell goods from their countries. Kate's mother and father had both worked at the 1892–1893 World's Fair in Chicago, before they knew each other. John Howison was a carpenter, helping to build the many buildings needed to house all the exhibits. Edna Dick had read a notice in the paper that a young girl with big brown eyes was needed to greet visitors in a restaurant. She got the job and her employer dressed her as Buster Brown. She would hand out postcards with a picture of herself in the costume. She had a lot of fun because all the adults thought she was adorable.

In 1933, Chicago held another World's Fair, and Kate and her mother went to Chicago to see it. It took them a whole day to reach Chicago on the train, so they were only able to spend one day at the fair. They stayed with Kate's grandmother, and though the fair was very large, they were very surprised to run into Kate's Aunt Jean and her cousin Ruth right inside the gates of the fairgrounds. Kate's Uncle Harold, her mother's brother, met them at the fair that night and took them to dinner at the Belgium Restaurant. (All the countries represented at the fair had restaurants to show off the cooking of their homeland.) Kate had a steak that was so rare it had to be sent back twice, but they all had a wonderful time anyway. One of the notorious attractions of the Fair was Sally Rand and her Fan Dance. Sally danced with two big pink ostrich fans and not much else. Her dance was talked about by all the men who had been to the Fair. Of course Kate's mother would not let her see it.

1933 was during the Great Depression and the Fair was a great help in creating lots of jobs for people and bringing more money into the city during those hard times. Residents of Chicago rented out rooms in their houses to visitors for 75 cents a night because hotels were so expensive.

WORLD'S FAIR
GAMES
SALLY RAND
BELGIUM RESTAURANT
CHICAGO 1933
Pedigo 9-19-90 ©

Ohio River Flood

In early 1937, the Ohio River overflowed and flooded large parts of Indiana and Kentucky. About one-fourth of New Albany was under water and a nearby town was almost completely flooded. Those people who had not escaped to higher ground had to be rescued from their roofs by canoe, rowboat, or powerboat. Kate's father, who was the General Freight Agent for the railroad, okayed the opening of freight cars loaded with small boats, food, and portable stoves, all necessary for the rescue operation. He brought home a two-burner gasoline stove and a country-cured ham for his family. He also brought home his boss's poodle, because his boss lived in a hotel where the lower floors were all flooded and there was no power, heat, or plumbing. The National Guard was called in to prevent the looting of houses that had to be abandoned. There was a 24-hour guard at the intersection by Kate's house for several days.

Meanwhile, it was still raining constantly, and things got worse. Finally, it turned cold again and started snowing. Everyone was asked not to shovel the snow because it would help hold some of the rainwater. This certainly made it hard to travel.

When the water receded, people went back to their homes and washed the mud out with garden hoses. These houses are now much sought after because some of the mud remained in the wood, which seems to discourage termites.

1937 Ohio River

Pedigo
7-23-90

53

"More Coffee Please"

When Kate grew up she married Tex Pedigo, the son of the Pioneer Lady pictured in the front of this book. Kate and Tex loved to travel in the wilderness. They would drive into the mountains and camp outdoors under canopies of trees. They built a fold-out bed into their car trunk, and would hang a tarp over the hood of the trunk in case it rained. They caught fish and cooked it in a skillet over an open fire. They made coffee in their "coffee can," a tin bucket with a chain to hang over a fire. One time a coyote licked Tex's face in the middle of the night while he was sleeping. It was a lot of fun and an adventurous way to travel.

Kate and Tex traveled all over the West, but they especially liked to travel in Alaska. The first year the Alaska Highway was complete, they drove all the way up to the very beginning. They also visited Mount McKinley the first year that the road there opened. By 1966, they had driven the Alaska Highway 18 times, and traveled every road in Alaska and the Canadian Yukon Territory.

This is a drawing of how Kate and Tex ate breakfast if the ground was too wet to sit on. Kate would get breakfast ready and Tex would set up the teeter-totter arrangement. Tex was much heavier than Kate so she was always up in the air. This way of eating kept them from getting wet, but it sure was hard to get coffee refills!

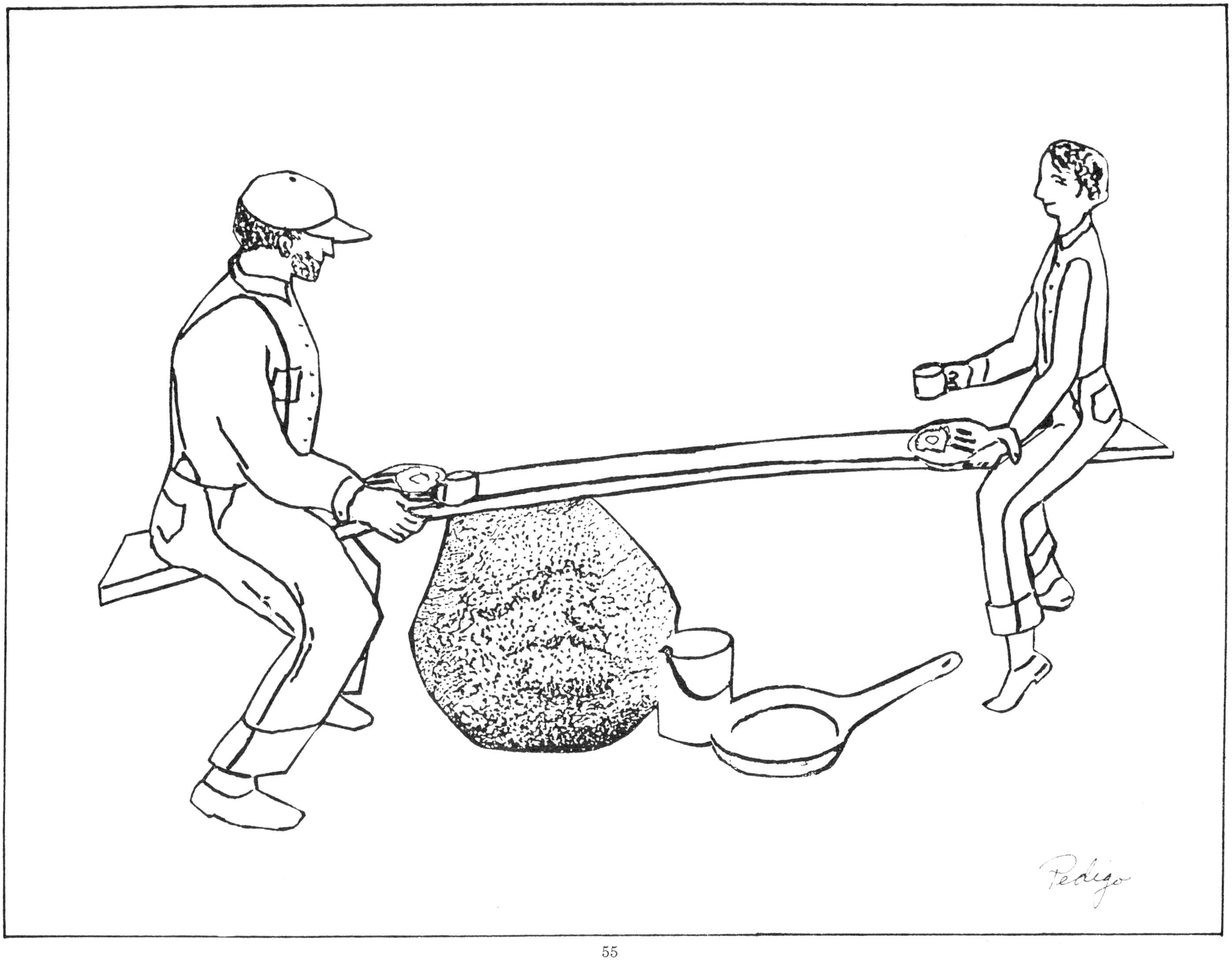
Pedigo

Company Picnic and Egg Toss

Kate visited her brother Donald and his wife Joyce in Kansas City in 1974. Donald worked for the International Harvester Company, and was sometimes transferred to different cities. Kate would visit him in each of the places he moved to. Her trip to Kansas City was a milestone. Now she had visited each one of the 50 states. During this trip, Kate went to a company picnic with Donald. The weather was very cold, even though it was June, and everyone had to eat indoors. Still, they went ahead and had an egg toss outside. In this game, everyone picks a partner and the partners stand across from one another in two long lines. Starting with one line, each person has to gently toss a raw egg to his or her partner. If the partner succeeds in catching it and keeping it intact, then he or she takes a step away and gently tosses the egg back. It was so cold that day everyone had to play in hats and mittens. This made the eggs slippery and hard to throw, so it was a very short game. The winners are the last couple with a whole egg. Needless to say, it was extremely messy, and Kate got all splattered.

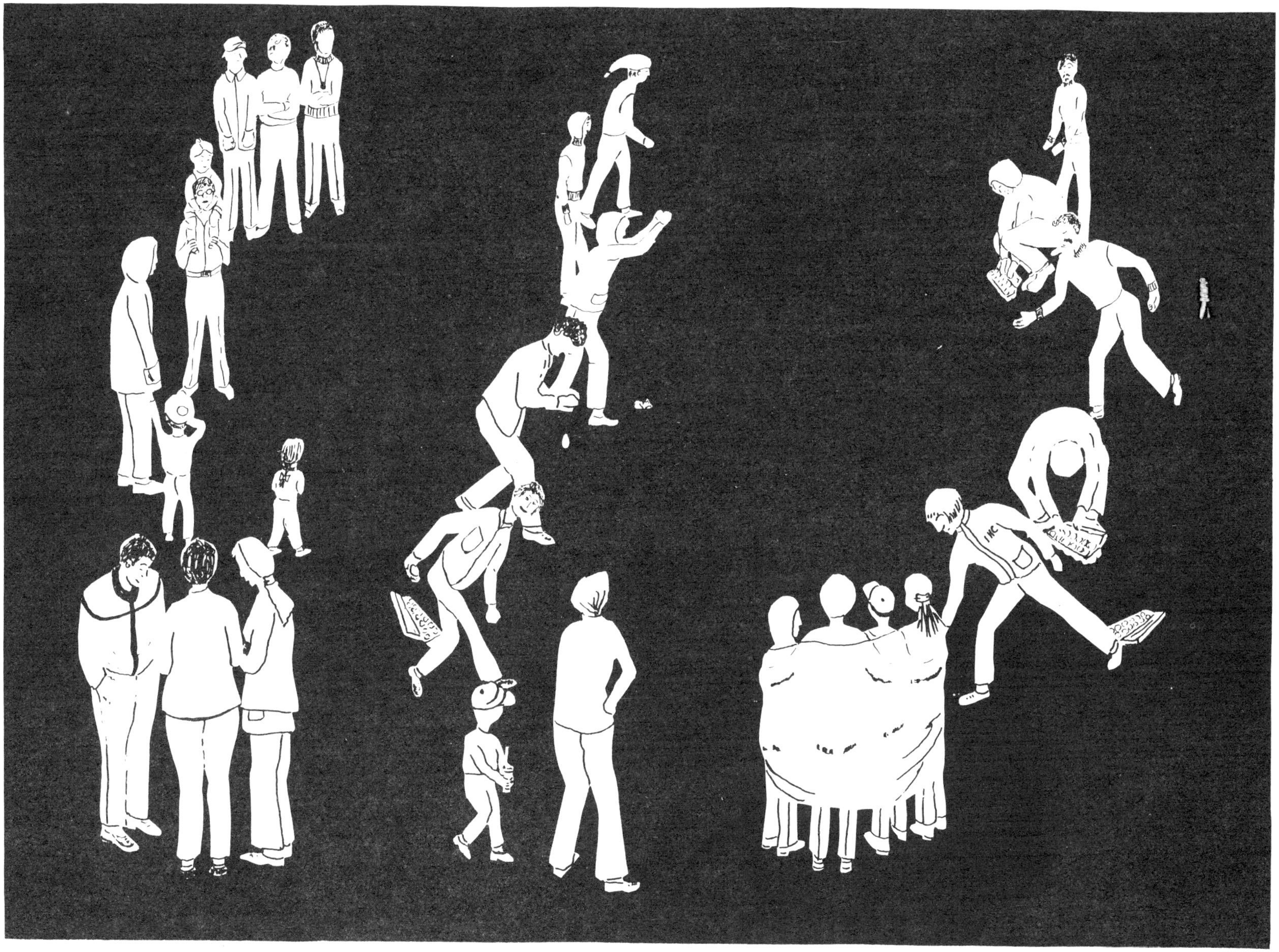

The Costume Party

In August, 1977, Kate spent three weeks in a summer art class in Banff Springs, Canada. The students held a costume party mid-way through the session. There were so many colorful and varied costumes that Kate made a drawing of the party. One of Kate's teachers had said there was "no such thing as a purple mountain" and therefore one of the other teachers came as a purple mountain. Another came as a cloud. One student came as a paintbrush, and another had a very good bird costume. Some of the costumes misfired. One of the men tried to dye his beard yellow, but it turned green instead. One man couldn't think of anything to wear so he put on a garbage bag for the party. Kate didn't have a costume; she put on a false face made out of a paint rag and wore a pajama suit with fake white ostrich feathers on the edge of the sleeves. It had started to snow, so she wore a sweater and warm pants underneath the pajamas. It was very strange weather for August.

59

Miss Maisano's Class

Now that Kate is a famous local artist, Miss Maisano, her neighbor, invites her to talk to her sixth grade class about art once a year.

Miss Maisano asks for volunteers to carry Kate's paintings into the classroom. Everyone holds up a hand, but only six are chosen. Kate then explains her techniques for painting and drawing. She adds that since she works from memory and doesn't have the subject (or model) to look at, it takes much longer. She tells the story behind each picture and lets the students ask questions. Kate wants the children to see that art is everywhere and tells them they should take art classes even if they are not "artistic." She assures them that they will use this knowledge in later life — it will affect their choices in home, car, clothing, and landscaping, and in entertainment, such as movies, TV, music, and theatre, even books and magazines.

Once the students asked Kate to draw a picture on the blackboard. She didn't have any thinking time so she did a scribble picture (something she frequently does for herself when she first gets an idea). When she finished, everyone knew the scribble picture described her morning in the classroom.

The next day the children all sent thank you notes with drawings of Kate's paintings. Many of them mentioned that their favorite was the Fire painting — the one showing the fire truck.

"Miss Maesano's Class"

About Kate

Kate (Kathryn Jeanette Howison Pedigo) was born August 2, 1911, to Edna Burr Dick Howison and John Alexander Howison. A female doctor came in a horse and buggy to Kate's parents' house in Joliet, Illinois, to supervise the birth. Kate's sister Ethleen had been born in 1904, and after Kate were three other siblings: Ardell (1913), Ruth (1917), and John Donald (1921).

When Kate was six, the family moved to New Albany, Indiana, where her father had a job as a general freight agent for the Kentucky and Indiana Terminal Railroad Company. Kate spent the rest of her childhood in New Albany, though the family moved several times within the town.

Kate took an art course in high school, but didn't like it. During a class on drawing in perspective, her teacher said her lines were as crooked as a "dog's hind legs." Kate liked French and math better, and went on to study chemistry for three years at the University of Louisville. When Kate left college, the country was in the middle of the Depression. She lost her first bank account (with only $14 in it) when the bank failed. It was also hard to find a job. For a while, Kate worked in a laboratory at the local hospital, then went to a hospital in Chicago to learn about blood chemistry. When she came home from Chicago, she went to work at the Federal Land Bank, which loaned money to farmers and farm corporations. Jobs there were better paying and Kate wanted the money to send her sister Ardell through business school.

In August, 1937, Kate traveled to California by train for a vacation. At the Los Angeles station, she looked out the train window and saw three men. Kate said jokingly to some friends, "One of those men is going to be my husband." It turned out to be an accurate prophecy. Kate was separated from her tour group in the crowded station. One of the three men, who happened to work for a taxi company, offered her a ride to the hotel to rejoin her group. His name was Tex Pedigo. He asked her out to dinner and spent the next three days showing her the sights of Los Angeles. On the third day he proposed marriage and she accepted. Kate continued on with her tour, going back to Indiana and her job for three months. She then returned alone to California, where she and Tex were married on November 19, 1937.

During their marriage, Kate and Tex spent much of their free time traveling together. They preferred Canada and Alaska to anywhere else. Tex did public relations work for the taxi company, and Kate would occasionally help him by greeting tours at the train station. She was a housewife the rest of the time. Tex soon became a vice-president in the company, and remained there until his retirement at age 75. He died three years later, in 1967. Kate then moved to northeast Los Angeles, a section called Eagle Rock, where she has lived ever since, becoming very active in community affairs.

Kate continued to travel, visiting South America by boat, going to New England to see the fall colors, and touring Europe several times by bus, even getting as far as Leningrad.

Although she loved to travel, she soon became a little bored and restless. A friend suggested she might enjoy taking up art as a hobby. Kate found that she did not necessarily have to be able to draw a straight line to create wonderful drawings. She first studied art in an Adult Education class, then two years later began taking part-time classes in painting, drawing, composition, and sculpture at the Otis Art Institute. She had many professors, her favorite being Sam Clayberger. Landscape and narrative painting and drawing were Kate's specialties. She has participated in many local shows and has won many awards.

Kate's biggest project to date is a series of murals of the history of Eagle Rock done for the City Hall. She organized the seven artists involved in the project and also painted one of the murals, showing Eagle Rock as it is today. Although it took only ten months to complete the murals, the group spent four years raising funds for the project.

Today Kate is involved in various art associations in California: a co-founder and board member of the Federation of Art Associations, editor of the Eagle Rock Art Association newsletter, board member of December Rose (an organization that encourages older adults to develop creative talents) and a member of the Verdugo Hills, Southland, and Beverly Hills Art Associations, the Hollywood Arts Council, and the Arroyo Arts Collective Group. She has worked as a show coordinator of local artists for six years and is also president of the Northeast Networkers (a group of small business people who have banded together to promote business), Secretary of the Eagle Rock Chamber of Commerce, and a member of the Eagle Rock Historical Society.

Photo Album

Delitha Cassandrew Jackson Pedigo, Pioneer Lady, 1893

Kate, 9 years old, 1920

Kate and Tex on the Alaska Highway

Samuel Madison Pedigo, 1893

Downtown New Albany under water after the Ohio River Flood, 1937

New Albany under water after the Ohio River Flood, 1937

LYRICS
for some of the favorite old songs everyone sang on the riverboats

My Old Kentucky Home
Lyrics and music by Stephen Foster

The sun shines bright in the old Kentucky home, 'Tis
summer, the darkies are gay; The
corn top's ripe and the meadow's in the bloom, While the
birds make music all the day; The
young folks roll on the little cabin floor, All
merry, all happy, and bright; By'n'
by hard times comes a knocking at the door, Then, my
old Kentucky home, good night!

CHORUS:
Weep no more, my lady, Oh! weep no more today! We will sing one song for the
old Kentucky home, For the old Kentucky home far away.

They hunt no more for the 'possum and the 'coon
On the meadow, the hill, and the shore;
They sing no more by the glimmer of the moon,
With sorrow where all was delight,
The time has come when the darkies have to part,
Then, my old Kentucky home, good-night!

REPEAT CHORUS

The head must bow and the back will have to bend,
Wherever the darky may go;
A few more days and the trouble all will end,
In the fields where the sugar canes grow;
A few more days for to tote the weary load,
No matter, 'twill never be light,
A few more days till we totter on the road,
Then, my old Kentucky home, good-night!

REPEAT CHORUS

Tiger Rag
by Harry DaCosta and D. J. La Rocca

Where's that tiger! Where's that tiger!
Where's that tiger! Where's that tiger!
Hold that tiger! Hold that tiger!
Choke him, poke him, kick him and soak him!
Where's that tiger? Where's that tiger?
Where oh where can he be?
Low or highbrow, they all cry now:
"Please play that Tiger Rag for me."

Beautiful Ohio
Lyrics by Ballard MacDonald; Music by Mary Earl

Long, long ago, Someone I know
Had a little red canoe
In it room for only two
love found its start,
Then on my heart
and like a flower grew.

CHORUS:
Drifting with the current down a moonlit stream
While above the Heavens in their glory gleam
and the stars on high Twinkle in the sky
Seeming in a Paradise of love divine
Dreaming of a pair of eyes that looked in mine
Beautiful Ohio, in dream again I see
Visions of what used to be.

Back Home Again In Indiana
Lyrics by Ballard MacDonald; Music by James F. Hanley

I have always been a wand'rer Over land and
sea, Yet a moonbeam on the water Casts a spell o'er
me A vision fair I see Again I seem to be: —

CHORUS:
Back home again in Indiana, And it seems that I can
see The Gleaming candlelight still shining bright Thru the
sycamores for me, The new mown hay — sends all its fragrance From the
fields I used to roam — When I dream about the moonlight on the
Wabash, Then I long for my Indiana home. Back home a-home.

Fancy paints on memry's canvas Scenes that we hold
dear, We recall them in days after Clearly they ap-
pear, And often times I see A scene that's dear to me: —

REPEAT CHORUS